PROFICIENT'S

GUIDE BOOK ON VSSF SPOT EXAM FOR
SPOT BASIC LEVEL, 2021

VSSF SPOT

BASIC LEVEL

BY

KAMAL SARMA
JAHNAVI SARMA

PROFICIENT

(A COMPLETE COACHING, DEVELOPMENT AND PRACTICE GUIDE)

Borjhar, VIP, Guwahati, Near North East small Finance Bank Branch, Assam, India-781015
Contact No. 9706567627, 9085094195,9101443160, Mail Id-kamalcaedcl@gmail.com

PREFACE

'PROFICIENT's Guide Book On VSSF SPOT Exam For SPOT Basic Level, 2021' is a comprehensive guide book for the students from Class III to Class V appearing the VSSF SPOT Exam conducted by Vikram Sarabhai Science Foundation(VSSF). This book is written under the guidance of the Academic scholars of Proficient Academy. The sole purpose of this book is to extend help and support to the students to gather conceptual knowledge of science and to make them understand how to appear the exam purposefully. We expect that the guidebook will be proved to be fruitful to share in depth knowledge with the students to solve the MCQ type questions. The readers are requested to send their feedbacks at the mail address of the author, so that we can improve the next editions. This book introduces you to how to present yourself in the examination. This book is not meant for learning the chapters, but to make the students understand the skill how to think logically and to find the right answers quickly. Again the SPOT Basic Level is for Class III to V only, but in this book we have included a few questions from VI standard too. It will help the students to answer the questions of higher standard than average. In some places the same questions are presented in different ways, so that the students can learn the art of understanding.

In this first edition 'Proficient' family tries to help the students with the questions related to the topics only, but no sample paper or introduction to the chapters are given in this book. But 'Proficient' is very much committed to improve the contents in the editions to come.

With best wishes to our readers and well wishers.

Authors
Kamal Sarma
Jahnavi Sarma

CONTENTS

SYLLABUS

SPOT BASIC-CLASS III TO V
2020-21

SUBJECT	WEIGHTAGE	TOPIC
SCIENCE	60%	Plants and animals, Birds, Water, Food Human Body, Matter and Materials, Light, sound and Force, Earth and Universe, Things around us, General Science, Earth Science
SPACE SCIENCE	20%	Topics shared post student registration. Shall be available in www.vssf.in
LOGICAL REASONING	10%	Basic IQ/Aptitude Test
ANALYTICAL THINKING	10%	

SPOT JUNIOR-CLASS VI TO VIII
2020-21

SUBJECT	WEIGHTAGE	TOPIC
SCIENCE	60%	Animals Kingdom, Plant Kingdom, Matter, Electricity, Earth Science, Magnets, Adaptations, Organisms and its behaviours, Transportation, Natural Resources, Metals and Non Metals, Materials, Forces of Nature, General Science of Living Around us, Nutrition, Agriculture, General and Applied Science.
SPACE SCIENCE	20%	Topics shared post student registration. Shall be available in www.vssf.in
LOGICAL REASONING	10%	Basic IQ/Aptitude Test
ANALYTICAL THINKING	10%	

SPOT SENIOR-CLASS IX TO X
2020-21

SUBJECT	WEIGHTAGE	TOPIC
SCIENCE	60%	Physics, Chemistry, Earth Science
SPACE SCIENCE	20%	Topics shared post student registration. Shall be available in www.vssf.in
LOGICAL REASONING	10%	Basic IQ/Aptitude Test
ANALYTICAL THINKING	10%	

SPOT BASIC-CLASS III TO V

SCIENCE

PLANTS AND ANIMALS

1. **Leaves are known as the food factory of the plant. What is the process by which plants make food is known as:**

      A.   Photosynthesis

      B.   Cytosynthesis

      C.   Mitosynthesis

      D.   Bio synthesis

Answer: **A.**   **Photosynthesis**

2. **Which is the largest animal on earth?**

      A.   Shark

      B.   Elephant

      C.   Blue whale

      D.   Giraffe

Answer: **C.**   **Blue whale**

3. **WWF is an international agency which helps to protect animals. WWF stands for:**

      A.   World wild life fund

      B.   Wild world family

      C.   World water forum

      D.   Wide wild fox

Answer: **A.**   **World wild life fund**

4. **Flying Reptiles were known as _________.**

A. Dinosaurs

B. Plesiosaurs

C. Pterodactyls

D. Brachiosaurus

Answer: C.   Pterodactyls

5. **Which of the following would best tell you if something is a living thing?**

A. It feels soft

B. It is green

C. It produces offspring

D. It soaks up water

Answer: C.   It produces offspring

6. **Dogs give birth to puppies; cats give birth to kittens. This process by which animals produce other animals of their kind is called:**

A. Reproduction

B. Germination

C. Metamorphosis

D. Polination

Answer: A.   Reproduction

7. **There are some organisms having both organs appearing in different parts of the body. Which of the following exhibits hermaphroditism?**

A. Snake

B. Chicken

C. Earthworm

D. Fly

Answer: C.   Earthworm

8. **Animals that live both on land and water are called?**

    A.   Amphibian

    B.   Aerial animal

    C.   Land Animal

    D.   Aquatic animal

Answer: A.   Amphibian

9. **Largest individual flower is from a plant known as ______**

    A.   Rhododendron

    B.   Amaryllis

    C.   Primrose

    D.   Rafflesia arnoldii

Answer: D.   Rafflesia arnoldii

10. **Animals that suckle their young one are called ____.**

    A.   Reptiles

    B.   Birds

    C.   Amphibians

    D.   Mammals

Answer: D.   Mammals

11. **What are animals, which eat both plants and animals, called?**

    A.   Herbivores

    B.   Insectivores

    C.   Carnivores

    D.   Omnivores

Answer: D.   Omnivores

12. **When a plant performs the process of photosynthesis what is produced?**

A. Carbon dioxide

B. Nitrogen

C. Oxygen

D. Green pigment

Answer: **C.** **Oxygen**

13. **Which of the following best represents one particular stage in a life cycle?**

A. A fish swimming

B. A seed sprouting

C. A leaf growing

D. A dog eating

Answer: **B.** **A seed sprouting**

14. **Largest Land based mammals on earth are _____**

A. Giraffe

B. Polar Bears

C. African Bush Elephant

D. Bison

Answer: **C.** **African Bush Elephant**

15. **Which is the strongest sense in a dog?**

A. Touch

B. Hearing

C. Smell

D. Taste

Answer: **C.** **Smell**

16. **What kind of organism comes last in every food chain?**

    A.   Omnivores

    B.   Consumers

    C.   Producers

    D.   Decomposers

Answer: D.   Decomposers

17. **A decomposer is an organism that**:

    A.   Preys on other animals

    B.   Eats only plants

    C.   Recycles nutrients

    D.   Uses sunlight to make food

Answer: C.   Recycles nutrients

18. **What is the role of a flower?**

    A.   Smell good

    B.   Look pretty

    C.   Make seeds

    D.   Make food for the plant

Answer: C.   Make seeds

19. **What process does an animal undergo when the sperm and egg cell unite?**

    A.   Life cycle

    B.   Fertilization

    C.   Reproduction

    D.   Hatching

Answer: B.   Fertilization

20. __________ is the second largest big cat species in the world.

> A. Tiger

> B. Jaguar

> C. Leopard

> D. Lion

Answer: D. Lion

21. **What do you call the spines and thorns of some plants which they use to protect themselves from danger?**

> A. Adaptive structure

> B. Camouflage

> C. Plant disease

> D. Enemies of plants

Answer: A. Adaptive structure

22. **Which group of animals has scales?**

> A. Mammals

> B. Amphibians

> C. Reptiles

> D. Birds

Answer: C. Reptiles

23. **Yeast is a type of ____.**

> A. Plant

> B. Animal

> C. Bacterium

> D. Fungus

Answer: D. Fungus

24.   **What is the name of a frog's young one?**

    A.   Infant

    B.   Puppy

    C.   Calf

    D.   Tadpole

Answer: D.   Tadpole

25.   **How do animals and humans release or give off water particles?**

    A.   Polination

    B.   Photosynthesis

    C.   Perspiration

    D.   Sterilization

Answer: C.   Perspiration

26.   **There are different species of animal and plants living together in the same environment. How is this organization classified?**

    A.   Class

    B.   Community

    C.   Section

    D.   Group

Answer: B.   Community

BIRDS

1.   **Birds have _____________ which are suitable for their eating habits.**

    A.   Beaks

    B.   Claws

    C.   Both

    D.   None of these

Answer: C.   Both

2.   **-------------- birds weaves grass to make a nest**

    A.   Weaver

    B.   Sparrow

    C.   Pigeon

    D.   Woodpecker

Answer: A.   Weaver

3.   **Which of the following is a seed eating bird?**

    A.   Vulture

    B.   Sparrow

    C.   Eagle

    D.   Woodpecker

Answer: B.   Sparrow

4.   **The baby birds grow inside the**

    A.   Eggs

    B.   Shelves

C.   Pupa

D.   Cupboard

Answer: A.   Eggs

5.   **Which of the following has strong curved beak**

A.   Crane

B.   Ostrich

C.   Parrot

D.   Pigeon

Answer: C.   Parrot

6.   **Which is the largest bird in the world**

A.   Emu

B.   Kiwi

C.   Ostrich

D.   Peacock

Answer: C.   Ostrich

7.   **_________________ can fly.**

A.   Ostrich

B.   Pigeon

C.   Emu

D.   Kiwi

Answer: B.   Pigeon

8.   **A ________make a hole in a tree trunk with its beak.**

A.   Penguin

B.   Sparrow

C.   Pigeon

D.   Woodpecker

Answer: D.   Woodpecker

9.   Which of the following has broad flat beak?

A.   Pigeon

B.   Sparrow

C.   Duck

D.   Woodpecker

Answer: C.   Duck

10.   Claws of flesh eating birds are called_________.

A.   Beak

B.   Toes

C.   Palms

D.   Talons

Answer: D.   Talons

11.   Birds do not have teeth, they have _______________.

A.   Tongue

B.   Muscle

C.   Beak

D.   Claws

Answer: C.   Beak

12.   Birds build _____________ when they have to lay eggs.

A.   House

B.   Nest

C.   Shed

D.   kennel

Answer: B.   Nest

13.   Eagles eat the ____________.

    A.   Seeds

    B.   Fruits

    C.   grass

    D.   Flesh

Answer: D.   Flesh

14.   Birds fly with their __________ .

    A.   Wings

    B.   Legs

    C.   Body

    D.   Fins

Answer: A.   Wings.

15.   Which bird makes caw caw sound?

    A.   Owl

    B.   Pigeon

    C.   Crow

    D.   Cuckoo

Answer: C.   Crow.

16.   Birds bodies are shaped like _____________.

    A.   Train

    B.   Bike

    C.   Aeroplane

    D.   Car

Answer: C.   Aeroplane

17. **Which one of the following is the smallest bird?**

    A.   Ostrich

    B.   Sparrow

    C.   Bee humming bird

    D.   Nightingale

Answer: **C.**   **Bee humming bird**

18. **Birds have _____________.**

    A.   Wings

    B.   Beaks

    C.   Eyes

    D.   All of these

Answer: **D.**   **All of these**

WATER

1. **Water is in the form of solid state is described as:**

   A. Vapor rising in the sky

   B.   Hail during a storm

   C. Waves crushing on the seashore

   D. Rain falling from the clouds

   Answer: B. Hail during a storm

2. **If one boils water it will convert into _____ .**

   A. Mist

   B. Steam

   C. Clouds

   D. Snow

   Answer: B. Steam

3. **Arvin lives near river side. Every day he throws kitchen wastes in the river. Unknowingly he is polluting which of the following resources?**

   A. Air

   B.   Water

   C. Soil

   D. All of these

   Answer: B. Water

FOOD

1.   **What two things can keep us healthy?**

   A.   A balanced diet and watching TV

   B.   A diet high in sweets and going swimming

   C.   Eating lots of fruit and vegetables and playing computer games

   D.   A balanced diet and exercise

Answer: D.   A balanced diet and exercise

2.   **The correct order of the following sequence (rabbit, fox, carrots, fungi) in a food chain would be:**

   A.   Carrots, fox, rabbit, fungi

   B.   Fungi, rabbit, fox, carrot

   C.   Carrot, rabbit, fox, fungi

   D.   Non of the above

Answer: C.   Carrot, rabbit, fox, fungi

HUMAN BODY

1. **The process of digestion ends in the :**

   A.   Food pipe

   B.   Small intestine

   C.   Large intestine

   D.   Stomach

   Answer: C.   Large intestine

2. **The soft part of the body is :**

   A.   Eyes

   B.   Bones

   C.   Muscles

   D.   Heart

   Answer: D.   Heart

3. **Which sense organ is used to tell if there is sugar in a glass of tea?**

   A.   Nose

   B.   Tongue

   C.   Skin

   D.   Ear

   Answer: B.   Tongue

4. **Which nutrient plays an essential role in muscle-building?**

   A.   Protein

   B.   Carbohydrate

   C.   Iron

D.   Fat

Answer: A.   Protein

5.   ____ helps pump blood through the entire body.

A.   Lungs

B.   Kidneys

C.   Heart

D.   Brain

Answer: C.   Heart

6.   X-ray is the method of taking images in the body. The branch of science dealing with it :

A.   Radiogram

B.   Radiology

C.   Radio wave

D.   Radiation

7.   Which of the following organs is also a muscle?

A.   The Kidney

B.   The Lungs

C.   The Heart

D.   The Brain

Answer: C.   The Heart

8.   Longest bone in human body is ________

A.   Femur

B.   Stirrup

C.   Tibia

D.   Fibula

Answer: A.   Femur

9.   **Who controls all the body parts?**

    A.   Brain

    B.   Stomach

    C.   Lungs

    D.   Kidneys

Answer: A.   Brain

10.   **Messages from all parts of the Body keep coming to the brain through our ___.**

    A.   Blood

    B.   Oxygen

    C.   Carbon-dioxide

    D.   Nerves

Answer: D.   Nerves

11.   **What kind of exercise helps the heart and lungs?**

    A.   Aerobic

    B.   Bowling

    C.   Weight lifting

    D.   Anaerobic

Answer: A.   Aerobic

12.   **People with lesser melanin have ____**

    A.   Lighter skin colour

    B.   Darker Skin colour

    C.   Does not influence skin colour

    D.   None of the above

Answer: A.   Lighter skin colour

13.   **The brain and nerves make up our ___.**

    A.   Digestive system

    B.   Nervous system

    C.   Skeletal system

    D.   Circulatory system

Answer: B.   Nervous system

14.   **Different organs together make an ___.**

    A.   Organ system

    B.   Skin

    C.   Brain

    D.   Muscles

Answer: A.   Organ system

15.   **Our skeleton is very important. Identify the function which is not supported by it**

    A.   Support the body

    B.   Protect the body

    C.   Communicate with the body

    D.   Helps the body move

Answer: C.   Communicate with the body

16.   **The framework of bones is called ___.**

    A.   Skeleton

    B.   Muscles

    C.   Kidney

    D.   Lungs

Answer: A.   Skeleton

17.   The _________________that takes the food from the mouth to the stomach.

    A.   Saliva

    B.   Wind pipe

    C.   Food pipe

    D.   Nerves

Answer: C.   Food pipe

18.   **How many bones are there in our body?**

    A.   206

    B.   300

    C.   375

    D.   208

Answer: A.   206

19.   **Which system removes the waste material from our body?**

    A.   Excretory

    B.   Nervous

    C.   Circulatory

    D.   Skeletal

Answer: A.   Excretory

20.   **The kidney throw out _____from our body.**

    A.   Water

    B.   Blood

    C.   Urine

    D.   Oxygen

Answer: C.   Urine

21.   **Intestines are the part of which organ system?**

A.	Circulatory

B.	Digestive

C.	Excretory

D.	Nervous

**Answer:	B.	Digestive**

**22.	How many times does a human heart beat in a day?**

A.	More than 10,000 times a day

B.	More than 1,00,000 times a day

C.	More than 1,000 times a day

D.	Around 2,00,000 times a day

**Answer:	B.	More than 1,00,000 times a day**

**23.	The heart, blood and blood vessels make up the-----**

A.	Respiratory system

B.	Nervous system

C.	Circulatory system

D.	Excretory system

**Answer:	C.	Circulatory system**

**24.	Stomach is the part of which organ system-**

A.	Nervous

B.	Digestive

C.	Respiratory

D.	Skeletal

**Answer:	B.	Digestive**

**25.	The nose, windpipe and lungs make up the -----**

A.	Respiratory system

B. Nervous system

C. Circulatory system

D. Excretory system

Answer: **A.** **Respiratory system**

26. **We inhale air through our -----**

A. Eyes

B. Lungs

C. Nose

D. Ear

Answer: **C.** **Nose**

27. **The -----takes food to all the parts of the body**

A. Lungs

B. Saliva

C. Heart

D. Blood

Answer: **D.** **Blood**

28. **The blood flows through pipes called**

A. Food pipe

B. Blood vessels

C. Wind pipe

D. Lungs

Answer: **B.** **Blood vessels**

29. **Which of the following helps us to taste?**

A. Ear

B. Stomach

C.   Nose

D.   Tongue

Answer: D.   Tongue

30.   Blood is pumped throughout our body by the

A.   Kidney

B.   Stomach

C.   Heart

D.   Lungs

Answer: C.   Heart

31.   If you are exposed to garbage, what kind of illness would you probably get?

A.   Heart failure

B.   Asthma

C.   Goiter

D.   Nose bleed

Answer: B.   Asthma

32.   Which of these minerals is needed by your bones?

A.   Calcium

B.   Protein

C.   Carbohydrates

D.   Vitamin A

Answer: A.   Calcium

33.   Which of the following are present in pairs

A.   Nose

B.   Stomach

C.   Lungs

D.   Mouth

Answer: C.   Lungs

34.   It allows you to bend your knees.

A.   Muscles

B.   Joints

C.   Femur

D.   Tendons

Answer: B.   Joints

MATTER AND MATERIAL

1. **Which among these clothing materials is synthetic material:**

    A.   Wool

    B.   Nylon

    C.   Silk

    D.   Cotton

Answer: **B.**   **Nylon**

2. **Recycling refers to:**

    A.   Burning trash completely

    B.   Burying trash in a landfill

    C.   Reducing the amount of waste over from using a product

    D.   Reusing a resource to make left something new

Answer: **D.**   **Reusing a resource to make left something new**

3. **Which of these classroom objects will a magnet most likely pick up?**

    A.   A rubber eraser

    B.   A plastic cup

    C.   Chalk

    D.   A metal paperclip

Answer: **D.**   **A metal paperclip**

4. **A mineral is a natural crystalline solid formed from geological process. Which among these not a mineral:**

    A.   Diamond

    B.   Wood

    C.   Gold

D.   Salt

Answer: B.   Wood

LIGHT, SOUND AND FORCE

1. **Which forms of energy are produced by a burning candle?**

    A.   Heat and mechanical

    B.   Electrical and sound

    C.   Light and Electrical

    D.   Heat and Light

Answer: **D.** **Heat and Light**

2. **Sound cannot travel through _______________**

    A.   Solid

    B.   Vacuum

    C.   Liquid

    D.   Air

Answer: **B.** **Vacuum**

3. **What do we call the objects that do not gives us light?**

    A.   Reflecting object

    B.   Non-luminous object

    C.   Luminous object

    D.   Non-living object

Answer: **B.** **Non-luminous object**

4. **Speed of light in vacuum is ________**

    A.   1,00,000 km/sec

B.   2,00,000 km/sec

C.   3,00,000 km/sec

D.   None of the above

Answer: C.   3,00,000 Km/sec

5.   **The outward force, away from the center, felt by an object in circular motion is**

___.

A.   Centripetal force

B.   Circular force

C.   Centrifugal forces

D.   Elastic force

Answer: C.   Centrifugal forces

6.   **We see _____________objects only when light fall on them.**

A.   Reflecting object

B.   Non-living object

C.   Luminous object

D.   Non-luminous object

Answer: D.   Non-luminous object

7.   **What are formed when an object blocks the path of light?**

A.   Images

B.   Rays

C.   Shadows

D.   Refractions

Answer: C.   Shadows

8.   **Our shadows are formed when we block the light from the__________.**

A.   Sun

B.   Table

C.   Chair

D.   Mirror

Answer: A.   Sun

9.   **A _______________is always formed on the opposite side of the light source**

A.   Circle

B.   Cube

C.   Shadow

D.   Mirror

Answer: C.   Shadow

10.   **Which of the following gives us light:**

A.   Sun

B.   Moon

C.   Satellite

D.   Comet

Answer: A.   Sun

11.   **What do we need to see things?**

A.   Heat

B.   Force

C.   Gravitational force

D.   Light

Answer: D.   Light

12.   **What is the main source of heat and light on Earth?**

A.   Sun

B.   Moon

C.   Stars

D.   Fire

Answer: A.   Sun

13.   The sun is the main source of heat and light of the living planet called __________.

A.   Jupiter

B.   Earth

C.   Venus

D.   Mars

Answer: B.   Earth

14.   **What do we call objects that give us light?**

A.   Matter

B.   Solid

C.   Non- Luminous

D.   Luminous

Answer: D.   Luminous

EARTH AND UNIVERSE

1. _______ is the most common element found in our universe.

    A.   Helium

    B.   Oxygen

    C.   Hydrogen

    D.   Nitrogen

Answer: C.   Hydrogen

2. **In our solar system the asteroid belt is found between ______ and _____.**

    A.   Mars and Jupiter

    B.   Earth and Mars

    C.   Jupiter and Saturn

    D.   Venus and Earth

Answer: A.   Mars and Jupiter

3. **How much % of oxygen is there in the air?**

    A.   78%

    B.   21%

    C.   1%

    D.   18%

Answer: B.   21%

4. **Which planet is known as the Morning and Evening Star?**

    A.   Earth

    B.   Mars

    C.   Venus

D.   Mercury

Answer: C.   Venus

5.   What do you call the imaginary line on which the Earth turns and which runs from pole to pole?

A.   Latitude

B.   Longitude

C.   Axis

D.   Equator

Answer: C.   Axis

6.   There are ... planets in our solar system.

A.   7

B.   8

C.   9

D.   10

Answer: B.   8

7.   How many natural satellites move around Earth?

A.   One

B.   Two

C.   Three

D.   Four

Answer: A.   One

8.   How many Earth days are equivalent to one day on the moon?

A.   15

B.   1

C.   365

D.	29

**Answer:	D.	29**

**9.	The biggest known volcano in our solar system is located on?**

A.	Moon

B.	Jupiter

C.	Saturn

D.	Mars

**Answer:	D.	Mars**

THINGS AROUND US

1.   __________ is used in balloons as it is lighter than air.

    A.   Helium

    B.   Oxygen

    C.   Nitrogen

    D.   Argon

Answer: A.   Helium

GENERAL SCIENCE

1.   _______ is the famous scientist who discovered gravity

    A.   Sir Issac Newton

    B.   Albert Einstein

    C.   Michael Faraday

    D.   None of the above

Answer: A.   Sir Issac Newton

2.   **What is another name for heat energy?**

    A.   Solar energy

    B.   Light energy

    C.   Electrical energy

    D.   Thermal energy

Answer: D.   Thermal energy

3.   _______ is the famous scientist known for inventing Telephone.

    A.   Thomas Alva Edison

    B.   Neils Bohr

    C.   Alfred Nobel

    D.   Alexander Graham Bell

Answer: D.   Alexander Graham Bell

4.   **Wright Brothers invented _______.**

    A.   Gun

    B.   Battle Tank

    C.   Ships

D.   Airplane

Answer: D.   Airplane

5.   _______ is the famous scientist who discovered Penicillin in 1928

A.   Sir Alexander Fleming

B.   Leonardo Da Vinci

C.   Michael Faraday

D.   Archimedes

Answer: A.   Sir Alexander Fleming

6.   What is a U-Boat?

A.   Ship

B.   Submarine

C.   Helicopter

D.   Balloon

Answer: B.   Submarine

7.   _______ is the inventor of Radio

A.   Guglielmo Marconi

B.   Thomas Edison

C.   Benjamin Franklin

D.   Michael Faraday

Answer: A.   Guglielmo Marconi

8.   What does a weather vane show?

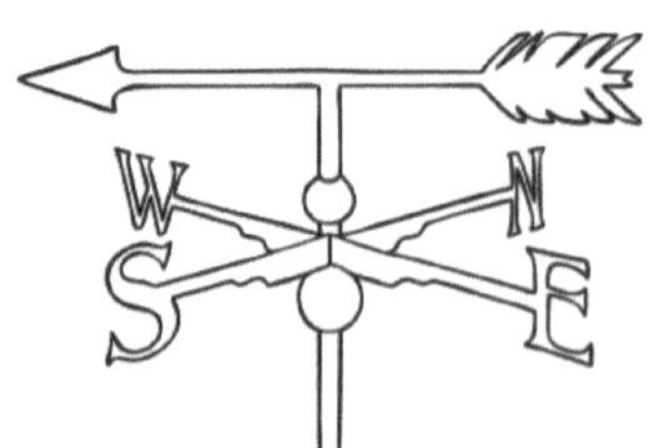

A.   Wind direction

B.   Air temperature

C.   Air pressure

D.   Cloud density

Answer: A.   Wind direction

9.   ________ is the famous scientist from Sweden, known as the inventor of dynamite.

A.   Thomas Alva Edison

B.   Neils Bohr

C.   Alfred Nobel

D.   Marie Curie

Answer: C.   Alfred Nobel

10.   The standard unit of measurement for energy is ____.

A.   Newton

B.   Ampere

C.   Watt

D.   Joule

Answer: D.   Joule

11.   Indian Science Congress 2020 was held in ______.

A.   New Delhi

B.   Lucknow

C.   Bengaluru

D.   Hyderabad

Answer: C.   Bengaluru

12.   **What instrument is used to measure wind speed?**

    A.   Thermometer

    B.   Speedometer

    C.   Anemometer

    D.   Barometer

Answer: C.   Anemometer

13.   **__________ was born on 15th September. This day is celebrated as Engineers Day in India.**

    A.   V Radhakrishnan

    B.   Sir M Visvesvaraya

    C.   Abdul Kalam

    D.   Satish Dhawan

Answer :   B.   Sir M Visvesvaraya

14.   **William Cullen made the first _______**

    A.   Air Conditioner

    B.   Refrigerator

    C.   Solar Water heater

    D.   None of the above

Answer :   B.   Refrigerator

15.   **What do we call the scientist that study about the soil?**

    A.   Meteorologist

    B.   Geologist

    C.   Pedologist

    D.   Psychologist

Answer: B.   Geologist

EARTH SCIENCE

1.	________ is the second most abundant element found on earth's crust.

    A.	Iron

    B.	Nickel

    C.	Cadmium

    D.	Silicon

**Answer:	D.	Silicon**

2.	The highest temperature ever recorded in Antarctica is 18.3 degree Celsius. The reading was taken by Esperenza research base of ________

    A.	Spain

    B.	Russia

    C.	Germany

    D.	Argentina

**Answer:	D.	Argentina**

3.	The movement of the earth on its axis is called:

    A.	Revolution

    B.	Rotation

    C.	Motion

    D.	Circle

**Answer:	B.	Rotation**

SPACE SCIENCE

1.   Mars is also known as the ___________ planet:

     A.   Green

     B.   Blue

     C.   Orange

     D.   Red

Answer: D.   Red

2.   **The moon is:**

     A.   Satellite

     B.   Plant

     C.   Round

     D.   Planet

Answer: A.   Satellite

3.   **The Moon produces no light, and yet it shines at night. Why is it so?**

     A.   The moon reflects the light from the Sun

     B.   The Moon rotates at a very high speed

     C.   The moon is covered with a thin layer of ice

     D.   The Moon has many craters

Answer: A.   The moon reflects the light from the Sun

4.   **Which is the closest planet to the sun?**

     A.   Venus

     B.   Mars

     C.   Mercury

D. Earth

Answer: **C.** **Mercury**

5. **Solar System is in ___________ galaxy.**

A. Milky Way

B. Andromeda

C. Proxima Centauri

D. None of the above

Answer: **A.** **Milky Way**

6. **________ is considered as father of Indian Space Program.**

A. Green C V Raman

B. Homi J Bhabha

C. Abdul Kalam

D. Vikram Sarabhai

Answer: **D.** **Vikram Sarabhai**

7. **The satellite known as artificial 'baby moon' is __________ :**

A. Apollo-8

B. Sputnik

C. Spot-6

D. Jupiter

Answer: **B.** **Sputnik**

8. **The first person to set foot on Moon__________.**

A. Albert Einstein

B. Neil Armstrong

C. APJ Abdul Kalam

D. Edmund Hillary

Answer: **B.   Neil Armstrong**

9.   **What is the largest asteroid in the solar system?**

A.   Moon

B.   Titan

C.   Ceres

D.   Forbes

Answer: **C.   Ceres**

10.   **Which planet is known as the Red Planet?**

A.   Earth

B.   Mars

C.   Venus

D.   Mercury

Answer: **B.   Mars**

LOGICAL REASONING

1. **Select the next number from the options below: 456:842::654:_____________.**

    A.   428

    B.   624

    C.   248

    D.   462

Answer: **C.**   **248**

ANALYTICAL THINKING

1.   **Tomorrow is Monday. What day was it seven days back?**

    A.   Sunday

    B.   Saturday

    C.   Monday

    D.   Tuesday.

Answer: A.   Sunday

2.   **David wanted to measure how fast different insects can crawl. He must have a ruler to help him find the speed. What other tool does he need to use?**

    A.   A clock with a second hand

    B.   A fan with different speeds

    C.   A long stick with a brush on the end

    D.   A thermometer with degrees Celsius

Answer: A.   A clock with a second hand

3.   **Which among these can avoid accidents at home?**

    A.   Keep the bathroom floor always wet

    B.   Toys, clothes and books should be left on the floor

    C.   Staircases should not have railings

    D.   Electrical switches should not be touched with wet hands

Answer: D.   Electrical switches should not be touched with wet hands

4.   **What does the following figure represent?**

A.   Pedestrian crossing

B.   Place where U-turns can be made

C.   Television

D.   Fax

Answer: **A.   Pedestrian crossing**

5.   **When the two even numbers are added, it becomes______________.**

A.   Even

B.   Odd

C.   None of the above

D.   Both A and B

Answer: **A.   Even**

6.   **Which of the following is a road safety measure?**

A.   Ignore traffic signals after midnight

B.   Drive under the influence of alcohol

C.   Overtake without using your indicator lights

D.   Wear a safety helmet while riding a motorcycle

Answer: **D.   Wear a safety helmet while riding a motorcycle**

7.   **There are two numbers. When you multiply them, the product is 6. Their sum is 5. What are the numbers?**

A.   3,2

B.   4,2

C.	2,2

D.	4,4

**Answer:	A.	3,2**

8.	**We should avoid which of these activities on a staircase:**

A.	We should rush down the staircase

B.	We should not be in a hurry

C.	We should not push other children

D.	We should climb the steps in a line

**Answer:	A.	We should rush down the staircase**

9.	**Aani can paint two pictures in an hour. How many hours will it take her to paint 8 pictures?**

A.	4 hours

B.	6 hours

C.	3 hours

D.	5 hours

**Answer:	A.	4 hours**

10.	**What time does the clock show?**

A.	12.15

B.	12.30

C.	3.00

D.   3.12

Answer: C.   3.00

11.   What time does the clock show?

A.   12.00

B.   7.00

C.   9.00

D.   6.35

Answer: B.   7.00

The End